W9-DHS-227

PREPARING TO RECEIVE HOLY COMMUNION

DEVOTIONS · PRAYERS · PSALMS · HYMNS
by Rev. Paul T. McCain

Based on F. J. Lankenau's *Communion Counsel and Prayers*

CONCORDIA PUBLISHING HOUSE · SAINT LOUIS

Published by Concordia Publishing House
3558 S. Jefferson Ave., St. Louis, MO 63118-3968
1-800-325-3040 • www.cph.org
Copyright © 2018 Concordia Publishing House

Manufactured in the United States of America

1   2   3   4   5   6   7   8   9   10   27   26   25   24   23   22   21   20   19   18

CONTENTS

Dedicated to my father, Rev. Paul B. McCain,
who administered Holy Communion
to me for the very first time

HOW TO USE THIS BOOK

The purpose of this book is to provide you with a resource you can use often as you prepare to receive the Lord's Supper. Keep it close by and refer to it as you consider the gift of the Lord's Supper in your life.

The chapters in this book are not intended to be read in any particular order, but are meant to provide you with devotional and doctrinal reflections, including quotations from the catechisms of Luther and from other places in the Lutheran Confessions and hymn stanzas to think about.

Additional resources are included in this little book to aid your Communion preparation—again, to be used as you choose. There are additional prayers, as well as seven psalms that throughout the Church's history have come to be referred to as the seven penitential psalms and have been used by countless generations of God's people to reflect on and confess their sin and to ask for God's mercy and forgiveness. Also included are a collection of classic hymns that you can read as devotional poems. They give voice to our deepest feelings about the Lord's Supper and help us reflect on the gifts there given. And finally, there is a series of questions and answers for Christians preparing to receive Communion. They were composed by Martin Luther.

But again, how you wish to use this little book is up to you. Read as many or as few of the devotions as you like, or use them as a springboard for further reflection and prayer on the gift of Holy Communion, the Blessed Sacrament of our Lord's true body and blood, given to you for forgiveness, life, and salvation.

> "Come to Me, all who labor and are heavy laden, and I will give you rest."
>
> Matthew 11:28

A Word to Those Preparing to Receive Holy Communion

As you prepare to receive the Lord's Supper, either for the very first time or yet again in a lifetime of receiving the Sacrament, the teaching, meditations, prayers, devotional thoughts, and hymn verses contained in this little book will assist you to approach the Lord's Table with reverent joy. There, you will receive, in trusting faith and confidence, your dear Lord Jesus' precious body and blood for forgiveness, life, and salvation. As with most things in life, it is easy to slip into a sort of "routine" and take the serious nature of communing for granted, growing indifferent to the tremendous blessings given by our Lord through His Sacrament. As you use the resources in this book, either all of some of them, it is our prayer that you will conclude your time of preparation eager to once more receive your Lord's sacred meal.

You are preparing to enter into the closest and most intimate relationship with your God and Savior. Such being the case, you will want to pray and seek God's rich blessings both before and after you commune. To this end, may you, like young Samuel, open your ears and heart and say: "'Speak, LORD; for Your servant hears' (1 Samuel 3:9). Grant me the knowledge of Your gracious truths and bless me with Your precious gifts of forgiveness, life, and salvation. Refresh my soul that I may see Your wondrous works and experience Your boundless love for me in Christ Jesus my Lord."

You have been faithfully instructed in the basic teachings of our Christian faith as revealed by God in the Holy Scriptures and as they are so simply and beautifully summarized by Dr. Martin Luther in his Small Catechism. As you examine yourself in light of God's Law, you realize you are indeed, by nature, a poor miserable sinner. There is no hiding from that reality, but—thank God—you do not need to hide in shame as Adam and Eve did when God came looking for them (Genesis 3). Rather, your Savior knows your sins and, out of pure love and mercy, came to this earth to live perfectly in your place and to take your place under the wrath of God, earning for you full forgiveness and reconciliation with God. You are a child of God. You are deeply loved by Him, and you have received His boundless grace, mercy, and peace, over and over again. You have also received instruction in the important work of the Holy Spirit through the Word and the Sacraments, and you have received His perfect work of regeneration and renewal. Some days you will feel that renewing grace more than other days, some days not all. Regardless of your feelings, the joyful blessings of the Sacrament are completely true for you every time you partake of it. This is a truth you will and can cling to in good times and bad—especially when life presses down on you, when you have failed and are feeling the guilt of your sin. So how best to prepare to receive this great gift? Let's discuss that.

First, you must not turn the reception of the Lord's Supper into a kind of "spiritual torture session" by which you subject yourself to endless introspection and try your very best to remember each and every mistake you have made and sin you have committed. While you can and must examine yourself and understand where you have sinned against God and your neighbor, the focus of your preparation for Holy Communion must be on the great gifts you are about to receive. Spend time meditating both on your great need for the Lord's mercy and on your Savior's deep and abiding love for you.

PRAYER

O blessed Jesus, as David says in the Psalms, "my sin is ever before me" (51:3). I thank and praise You that You so lovingly invite me to come to You with my weaknesses and heavy burdens so that You can give me rest. You have redeemed me, and in Holy Baptism, You gave me the blessings of Your redemption, accepted me as Your own, and made me the heir of life everlasting. You have until now graciously kept me in body and soul. Now, You are about to add another unspeakably great blessing to all the other innumerable tokens of Your love. Your will is to unite Yourself most intimately and mysteriously with me by giving me Your own true body and blood under the consecrated bread and wine of Holy Communion.

O Lord Jesus, I feel my unworthiness and realize how often I have sinned and fallen short of Your holy will for me. I pray, therefore, that You will open my eyes more fully to see the wonders of Your grace. Give me a greater understanding that I may know even more the depths of Your love.

And after having partaken of Your precious body and blood, let me be Yours more fully in mind and body. Let me cling more firmly to the precious assurance of Your grace, and enlarge my heart more perfectly in love toward You and my neighbor. Grant me an increase of joy and peace and a greater measure of courage to confess You before others by the testimony of my lips and the deeds of my hands. Yes, blessed Jesus, grant that my whole life may be a recognition that You are my Lord, and help that my greatest joy may consist in serving You. Lord Jesus, here am I—let me be Yours forever, Yours alone. Amen.

What the Lord's Supper Is

Luther's Small Catechism says the Lord's Supper "is the true body and blood of our Lord Jesus Christ under the bread and wine, instituted by Christ Himself for us Christians to eat and to drink" ("What is the Sacrament of the Altar?"). With these simple words, you are told what Christ gives you in His Holy Supper. These words from the Catechism are based on Christ's own words as found in Matthew 26:26–28; Mark 14:22–24; Luke 22:19–20; and 1 Corinthians 11:21–25. Jesus' words from these passages are also used to bring us His promises whenever we receive Holy Communion (see, for instance, *LSB*, p. 162).

When Christ instituted this Holy Sacrament, He took bread and wine and told His disciples to eat and drink these visible elements; but He also explicitly declared that under the bread and wine, they were also receiving His true body and blood; for He says, to use His own words: "This is My body, which is given for you. . . . This cup is the new testament in My blood, which is shed for you for the forgiveness of sins" (*LSB*, p. 162). There is no truth more plainly expressed in Scripture than that Christ gives you His real body and blood under the bread and wine to eat and to drink. So plainly is this truth expressed that nobody can possibly go wrong by simply clinging to Jesus' words. Our Lutheran Confessions elsewhere explain it like this:

> In the Lord's Supper, Christ's body and blood are truly and actually present. They are administered with those things that are seen, bread and wine. And we speak of the presence of the living Christ, for we know that "death no longer has dominion over Him" (Romans 6:9). (Apology of the Augsburg Confession X 57)

Our Lord guided the writers of Scripture to record these word not once, not twice, but four times. This was done to make infinitely clear that Jesus wants these words to be accepted in their simple and ordinary sense. But not even satisfied with this repetition, the Holy Spirit inspired the apostle Paul to write, "The cup of blessing that we bless, is it not a participation in the blood of Christ? The bread that we break, is it not a participation in the body of Christ?" (1 Corinthians 10:16). This can only mean that the very body that was given for us on the cross and the very blood that was shed for your redemption are united with the bread and wine as you receive these earthly elements in the Holy Supper.

And so, be ever mindful that you are not receiving just bread and wine in the Lord's Supper. Nor is it the case that bread and wine are merely symbols that remind you of Christ's body and blood; for if that were the case, there could be no actual communion of bread and the body of Christ or of wine and the blood of Christ in the Sacrament. On the other hand, it is equally clear that bread and wine are not changed into Christ's body and blood so that they lose their original nature and properties; for in that case, it would also be impossible to speak of a communion, that is, a uniting of the bread with Christ's body or of the wine with Christ's blood in this Supper.

In some mysterious manner, altogether beyond human understanding, a union of the body and the blood of Christ under the bread and wine takes place in the Holy Sacrament, so that when you, with your mouth, receive the consecrated bread and wine, you are receiving the crucified and risen Lord's actual body and blood. Every communicant therefore can say with all confidence and joy, "I have eaten Christ's real body and drunk His real blood."

Christ says: "This is My body, which is given for you. . . . This cup is the new testament in My blood, which is shed for you for the forgiveness of sins" (*LSB*, p. 162). Keep sight of these words, since they so very clearly express the blessed truth that in the Sacrament you receive the body that was given and the blood that was shed for your redemption, and they can thus only make you firmer in your faith that you receive Christ's true body and blood in Holy Communion.

Of course, this is all beyond human power to understand; for how can our limited minds comprehend this incomprehensible mystery? But do not let this trouble you, since it is your kind and loving Savior, your true and ever faithful Jesus, the all-wise and almighty Lord, who assures you of the real presence of His body and blood under the bread and wine in the Sacrament? Why worry about understanding this impenetrable mystery as long as you know that it is just as the kind Lord Jesus says?

PRAYER

Dearest Jesus, Your truthful lips assure me that in the blessed Sacrament You give me Your body and Your blood under the bread and wine. I am fully satisfied with Your assurance, and I trust Your Word in which You declare Your actual presence—though my reason cannot comprehend it. Yes, Lord Jesus, all thanks and praise are Yours, for You give me Your true body and blood in the Sacrament—the same body that was given for me on the cross, and the same blood that was shed for my sins and transgressions—for Your Word is more certain to me than my understanding and more valuable to me than all my limited experience. I pray You, keep me in this faith by Your Holy Spirit for Your mercy's sake. Amen.

Faithful Preparation
for Holy Communion

The Lord's Supper is no ordinary meal. It is even far above the richest banquet a king might prepare for some honored guest; for in it, you are given Christ's true body and blood under the visible elements of bread and wine. Indeed, you are the guest and Christ Jesus your gracious host who brings you into the banquet of salvation by clothing you with the robe of His righteousness that He won for you by His perfect life and innocent, atoning suffering and death on the cross and through His glorious resurrection.

When the Lord descended in the cloud and passed before Moses, Moses bowed his head and worshiped (Exodus 34:6, 8). Here in the Lord's Supper, however, you do not merely see the Lamb of God, but you also receive Him—His body and blood. When Uzzah (2 Samuel 6:6–7) put his hand on the ark of the covenant, which only priests and Levites were allowed to touch, he immediately died; how much more should you want to be careful so that you do not eat and drink judgment to yourself by unworthy partaking of the bread and wine in the Lord's Supper, since here's the real body, of which the ark was only the shadow!

> Whoever, therefore, eats the bread or drinks the
> cup of the Lord in an unworthy manner will
> be guilty concerning the body and blood of the
> Lord. Let a person examine himself, then, and
> so eat of the bread and drink of the cup.
>
> 1 Corinthians 11:27–28

Such an honest examination will bring out your weaknesses and unworthiness, your sinfulness and damnableness, and show you that you deserve God's wrath and punishment in time and eternity.

But as you come to a realization of your own unworthiness and vileness, the goal is not simply to feel the guilt of your sin, or worse, to wallow in some kind of "spiritual pity party." No, rather, the Holy Spirit uses the Holy Law of God as a mirror for you to see the accurate reflection of who you are. And thus, aware of your great need, you will be moved to desire even more deeply the body and blood of the beloved Son of God, your precious Jesus, your Lord and Master who has so lovingly bestowed the gift of His Holy Supper on you. He gives you so freely of His mercy. Of this, you are assured by the blessed bread and cup, which are the communion of the body and blood of the very Lamb of God, who takes away the sins of the world and whose very body and blood are given you in the Sacrament. Surely, He who makes you a partaker of His body and blood cannot wish you harm. Accept this blessed truth in childlike faith and say, "God would be merciful to me, a sinner, and to this end He gives me the very body and blood that gained my forgiveness. In the Holy Sacrament, He gives me all the blessings of Christ's redemption, forgiveness of sins, life, and salvation."

PRAYER

O Lord God, heavenly Father, I know I am most sinful and unworthy, and Your all-seeing eye can behold even more than is revealed to me. I am not worthy to be called Your child and would not dare to do so if You, in Your un-limited grace, did not assure me of my acceptance as Your child in spite of all my disobedience. I am mindful of the words of the centurion, "Lord, I am not worthy to have You come under my roof, but only say the word, and my servant will be healed" (Matthew 8:8). So, also, I see how unworthy I am to come to the Table You have prepared for us and where You will give us the body and blood of Your Son under the earthly elements of bread and wine. It is only the assurance of Your Word that I am a welcome guest that gives me courage to come with all my sins and unworthiness. Yes, it is because I trust in Your grace and in Jesus' atonement for my sins that I come just as I am, poor and wretched, seeking the riches of Your forgiveness and the comfort of Your love. Grant that I may receive the blessings I humbly and believingly seek, for the sake of Jesus Christ, my Lord and Savior. Amen.

The Beneficial Use
of the Lord's Supper

In His Holy Supper, the Lord Jesus gives you the most precious treasures. He there grants you gifts without which you would be lost for all eternity. The gifts He gives open the gates of paradise to you and grant you a share in the eternal joy and the home He has gone to prepare for you. When He instituted His Supper, He whose lips cannot lie declared: "This is My body, which is given for you. . . . This cup is the new testament in My blood, which is shed for you for the forgiveness of sins" (*LSB*, p. 162). Not only do you orally receive Christ's body and blood, but as you receive these in, with, and under the consecrated bread and wine with your mouth, you also receive by faith what His words declare, namely, the forgiveness of sins. Were you merely to receive Christ's body and blood with your mouth, it would have been sufficient for Him to have said, "This is My body; this is My blood." But He says more. Not only does He tell you that He gives you His body and blood, but because it is His body and blood you are receiving, you are therefore receiving the fruits of His great saving work on the cross for you.

The Lord Jesus not only desires that you eat His body and drink His blood, but precisely because it is His body and blood you are receiving, He also invites you to trust that His body was given for you and His blood was shed for you for the remission of your sins; yes, He seals and emphatically confirms this by giving you to eat and drink the very body and the very blood that merited this forgiveness for you. And you know that where there is forgiveness of sins, there is also life and salvation. These are the precious treasures Christ gives you in the Holy Supper, and without these you should be forever lost—but through them, you are made an heir of heaven. These treasures, imparted to you in the Sacrament by the word of promise, make you rich and eternally happy.

And all this is given us without money and without price; for no merit or worthiness on your part is expected or demanded. What the labor of your hands cannot do, what your gold and silver cannot buy, Christ gives you freely in the Sacrament—forgiveness of sins, life, and salvation.

But what if you have doubts? And we all do from time to time. How best to work through these doubts? When doubts arise, then, more than ever, it is time to devote yourself to the Lord's words of promise, the great "given . . . [and] shed for you." After examining yourself once again according to the holy standard of God's Law, you recognize your great need and look to the crucified Savior, reflecting on the great love that so moved Him to offer Himself up for your sins and the sins of the entire world. Such thoughts will then fill your heart with gratitude and cause your lips to overflow with praise to God for the priceless riches He bestows on you in His Supper. This humble and believing contemplation of God's love will then lead you to regard the Sacrament as a true Eucharist, an act of thanksgiving, and cause you whole-heartedly to join in singing: "It is truly good, right, and salutary that we should at all times and in all places give thanks unto You, holy Lord, almighty Father, everlasting God" (*LSB Altar Book*, p. 145). And after partaking of Holy Communion, you shall heartily pray: "We give thanks to You, almighty God, that You have refreshed us through this salutary gift, and we implore You that of Your mercy You would strengthen us through the same in faith toward You and in fervent love toward one another; through Jesus Christ, Your Son, our Lord, who lives and reigns with You and the Holy Spirit, one God, now and forever" (*LSB*, p. 166).

God grant that you may thus believingly and gratefully partake of the Lord's Supper at all times!

PRAYER

Almighty and eternal God, I am about to approach the Table prepared for me by Your dear Son, my Lord Jesus Christ. I come as one who is sick, to find healing; as one unclean, to be cleansed; as one blind, to receive sight; as one poor, to be made rich. I pray You, grant that I may find healing, cleansing, sight, and riches; help that I may humbly and reverently, with due sorrow and devotion and childlike faith, approach the Holy Sacrament and thus receive Christ's body and blood unto my salvation and ever be numbered among the members of His spiritual Body in time and eternity. Also help that I may so use the Sacrament that the fruits of Christ's redemption may be shown in my daily life to the praise of His holy name. I ask this for Jesus' sake. Amen.

Why Did Christ Institute the Sacrament?

In Holy Communion, Christ gives you His body and blood under the bread and wine for the forgiveness of your sins. As you use the external, visible elements according to His institution, you are made partakers of His grace and salvation. By uniting His transcendent blessings with the earthly elements, His purpose is to come to your assistance and aid to help you, and you will particularly sense this when your faith is weak and faltering, when you feel deeply a particularly painful experience, or when you feel the burden of guilt for a sin you have committed that troubles you profoundly, either recently or one that is brought to your mind often from your past. "Casting all your anxieties on Him, because He cares for you" (1 Peter 5:7)—this is demonstrated so remarkably as He gives you His body and blood. The very blood of Christ, which was shed to institute and confirm the new covenant of grace, is given to you in the Lord's Supper as a lasting memorial of His atoning death upon the cross. As often as you eat the bread and drink the cup in Holy Communion, you show forth the Lord's death; that is, you declare that He died for you and all sinners and that His death is in full effect until the end of days. The Lord's Supper is a constant reminder to you of Christ's vicarious and atoning death.

> They should regard and use the Sacrament just like a precious antidote against the poison that they have in them. Here in the Sacrament you are to receive from the lips of Christ forgiveness of sin. It contains and brings with it God's grace and the Spirit with all His gifts, protection, shelter, and power against death and the devil and all misfortune.
>
> (Large Catechism, part V, paragraph 70)

The Lord Jesus expresses the purpose of the Lord's Supper very plainly Himself in the words "given . . . [and] shed for you for the forgiveness of sins" (*LSB*, p. 162). By these blessed words, the Savior tells you that His body was given into death that you might live and that His blood was shed that you might be cleansed from your iniquities. He wants you to eat His body and drink His blood that you may live eternally. Oh, how much your Savior loves you. He is looking for every opportunity to secure your salvation and fill you with joy and peace inexpressible, that peace that passes all understanding, which does and will guard your heart and your mind until life everlasting. Prayerfully ponder your dear Savior's precious intentions for you in His Supper as you approach His Table. Consider His tender care for you by connecting His grace with the visible elements in the Sacrament. When doubts press heavily, look to your Savior and see there again His great love for you, and then come to His Holy Meal. Remember that it is the blood of the new testament, or new covenant, that Christ gives you in the Sacrament; for it is just this fact that should assure you of His grace.

> Jesus, priceless treasure,
> Fount of purest pleasure,
>   Truest friend to me!
> Ah, how long in anguish
> Shall my spirit languish, Yearning Lord, for Thee?
>   Thou art mine,
>   O Lamb divine!
> I will suffer naught to hide Thee,
> Naught I ask beside Thee.

LSB 743:1
Johann Franck; tr. Catherine Winkworth

PRAYER

O Lord Jesus, how unspeakably You love me and how earnestly You long for my happiness and salvation! You gave Yourself into death, into shameful death, even into death upon the cross, to atone for my sins and to make me acceptable in the eyes of Your Father. But You desired to do still more—Your boundless grace has prompted You to give me in Your Holy Sacrament further proof of Your all-absorbing interest in my welfare in order to strengthen my weak faith and confirm the covenant of Your grace. In this Sacrament, You impress on me that I should never forget Your death for my salvation.

I cannot sufficiently thank You for Your goodness, since it is impossible for me to measure its height or depth, its length or breadth; but I pray that You help me so that I may at least in a small measure see and acknowledge Your boundless love as I approach Your Table. Strengthen my weak faith and give greater ardor to my love for Your mercy's sake. Amen.

THE BENEFIT OF HOLY COMMUNION

Christ, the loving Savior and almighty God, has spread for you a rich and blessed banquet in the Holy Supper. All the blessed fruits of His redemption He there sets before you for your benefit. By His boundless love, He not only assures you of your redemption in the Gospel, but also in the Sacrament actually communicates to us the very body and blood given and shed for our salvation.

> "Take and eat, this is my body."
> This word is the whole gospel.
>
> AE 36:288

This unlimited grace should be ever in your thoughts as you approach His Table, so that you will always remember that all His merits, the whole fruit of His redemption, are there offered, given, and sealed to you. The simple acceptance of the Savior's words in which He tells you that He gives you His body and blood—the very body and blood given and shed for the forgiveness of your sins—gives you this blessed assurance. In the Sacrament, you eat the very body that was nailed to the cross and that died for your transgressions, and you drink the very blood that was shed for the atonement of your sins. In giving you His true body and blood, Christ gives you all that He gained for you by His suffering and death. In other words, Jesus and His atonement, His perfect holiness and righteousness, His merits and full redemption, are fully and freely given to you in the Lord's Supper. Here is indeed grace above measure and love beyond comprehension. But it is really and truly just as we have said; for Christ's own words in unmistakable language assure you of the blessed fact.

A further special benefit derived from the Lord's Supper is that you are assured of a most intimate communion with all believers on earth; for at the Lord's Table, all Christians partake of the one bread and the one cup. No matter how great a distance of space, race, language, or condition in life may separate you from other believers, in the Holy Supper there is an invisible but indissoluble tie, a tie that binds all believers of all times and places together in the one faith in the one Savior. Think of the ones whom you love and cherish who have gone on before to be with the Lord, and recognize that you are receiving the Lord's body and blood while they in heaven are rejoicing in His immediate presence, as we all look forward to His coming on the great and Last Day when He will raise us and all believers to be with Him for all eternity in the new heavens and new earth. Indeed, as we sing in the communion liturgy:

> Therefore with angels and archangels and with
> all the company of heaven we laud and mag-

nify Your glorious name, evermore praising You and saying: Holy, holy, holy, Lord God of pow'r and might: Heaven and earth are full of your glory. Hosanna. Hosanna. Hosanna in the highest. Blessed is He who comes in the name of the Lord. Hosanna in the highest.

LSB Altar Book, pp. 164–65

All the spiritual possessions of Christ and his saints are shared with and become the common property of him who receives this sacrament. Again all sufferings and sins also become common property; and thus love engenders love in return and [mutual love] unites.

AE 35:51

And as you partake of Holy Communion, your faith is strengthened by the gift of grace given, so your love toward God and fellow man is strengthened and increased. Without Jesus, you cannot truly love and serve God and your neighbor; but as you are further united with Jesus, you will grow in your love toward others and will earnestly desire to give expression through good works of your great thanks and praise of your loving Savior, who so graciously gifts you with forgiveness, life, and salvation in His Holy Supper.

And finally, receiving the body and blood of your victorious and exalted Savior increases and fosters your hope and confidence of having life eternal in Him. In receiving Christ's body and blood, you cannot but be confirmed in your trust that He will not fail to fulfill for you His promise: "I go to prepare a place for you" (John 14:2) and "Where I am, there will My servant be also" (John 12:26).

Look how marvelous are the blessings and gifts your Savior gives you in His Holy Supper—so great and precious, indeed, that they are your highest joy and greatest pleasure in this life! Is not the grace there offered rich beyond measure?

PRAYER

Dearest Jesus, in Your Holy Supper, You have prepared a feast that is able to supply all the wants of my soul; here, You would give me food and drink to strengthen my weak faith, to impart new strength to my love, and to enliven my hope of life everlasting. Grant me an increased measure of Your Holy Spirit so that by the enlarging of my faith I may more fully partake of the riches You would impart to me in Your Holy Supper. Hear my prayer for Your love's sake. Amen.

WHEN YOU DO NOT FEEL LIKE COMMUNING

Jesus says: "Blessed are you who are hungry now, for you shall be satisfied" (Luke 6:21). This is also true for you when you go to the Lord's Supper with a hungry and thirsty soul. When you hunger after righteousness, you will experience that Christ is the fount of all blessing. You will taste and see that the Lord is good.

> Jesus said to them, "I am the bread of life; whoever comes to Me shall not hunger, and whoever believes in Me shall never thirst. But I said to you that you have seen Me and yet do not believe. All that the Father gives Me will come to Me, and whoever comes to Me I will never cast out. For I have come down from heaven, not to do My own will but the will of Him who sent Me. And this is the will of Him who sent Me, that I should lose nothing of all that He has given Me, but raise it up on the last day. For this is the will of My Father, that everyone who looks on the Son and believes in Him should have eternal life, and I will raise him up on the last day."
>
> John 6:35–40

But what about those times when you do not feel like communing? It is not that you despise it, but you may find yourself feeling cold and indifferent. What are the causes for this? What can you do at times like this? Certainly, if you are feeling like not taking Holy Communion, it is not the Lord's fault. It is not because He has failed you, but rather that you have somehow failed Him. Consider what may be causing you to feel this spiritual coldness and indifference. Your desire and your hunger for Him feels weak and may even fail at times. Jesus Christ is the same yesterday, today, and forever. His supplies are as plentiful now as they were two thousand years ago, and He will continue to offer you a full and rich supply to the end of time. His Table is ever ready, and it is richly furnished to satisfy your hungry soul. But you find yourself hesitant and lacking in spiritual appetite.

What is the cause of this lack of hunger on your part? Why this indifference to the rich banquet spread for you in the Lord's Supper? You do not appreciate God's grace because you are blind to the hideousness of your sin. You do not long for the assurance of God's pardon because the damnableness of your transgression is not before you. You do not long for the fullness of Christ's mercy because you do not feel empty. You do not seek amnesty from the King of kings because you do not recognize that you are guilty of treason. You have no desire for the garments of Jesus' righteousness because you do not see your shameful nakedness caused by sin. You have no longing to be washed in the fountain of Jesus' blood because you are ignorant of your filthy, dirty condition as you stand before His perfect holiness and righteousness.

Oh, that God would give you hunger. May God make you truly hungry so that you do not perish for want of Christ, as is the case with thousands. Yes, may Christ make you truly hungry, so that, in giving you His own body to eat and His blood to drink, He can fill and strengthen you! He longs to enlarge the desire of your soul. He would not have you be content with crumbs; no, He would give you a seat at His lavish banquet of salvation. His hand is overflowing with riches; may your hand be held out to receive the treasures intended for you! While the dear Savior has already given you more than you had a right to ask, He desires that you want even more still. He yearns to have you say: "I long to come into ever fuller possession of the riches of Christ's grace, to know Him and His will better, to appropriate Him with all His merits more fully, and to serve Him more loyally."

Luther once marveled at the sweet and saving swap Jesus continues to give us in the Lord's Supper in this way:

> For Christ and I are being baked into each other in such a way that my sins and death become His

and His righteousness and life become my own. In short, a most blessed exchange is taking place here.

(Sermon for Maundy Thursday [April 13, 1525], WA 17/1:175.8–11, translated by John R. Stephenson)

If we come thus hungry to His Table, the all-gracious and bountiful Savior will surely say to us: "Ask whatever you wish, and it will be done for you" (John 15:7) and "Open your mouth wide, and I will fill it" (Psalm 81:10).

PRAYER

Lord Jesus, make me truly hungry for Your love, which I do not merit, but of which You would make me more certain in Your Holy Supper. Fill me ever with longing for the food and drink of life to which You have so tenderly invited me; and as I partake of Your body, which languished for me on the cross, and drink of Your blood, which was shed for my sins, may I never forget Your love, dear Savior! Jesus, bread of heaven, nourish my weak faith with Your strength. Savior, fount of every blessing, increase my love for You and my fellow men. O Lord God, grant my humble prayer for my good and Your glory! Amen.

Obstacles to Receiving
Holy Communion

You know your heart and mind should be centered on your Savior and the great blessings He gives you in His Sacrament, but there comes to mind other thoughts, concerns, sorrows, and worries about earthly matters that weigh heavily on you and may deprive you of the great joy and blessing of the Sacrament and distract you from it. If you permit Satan to fill your heart with doubts as to God's help and protection in earthly things, how can you rest securely in the thought that, in the Holy Supper, Jesus will make you a partaker of all His merits? If you cannot trust God to care for your body, how can you have confidence in Him to provide for the wants of your soul? But, thanks be to God, you can trust the Lord for the little things, and then you can and will rely on Him for heavenly and eternal blessings. It is therefore necessary to permit the Savior's blessed assurances of His abiding help to drive from your heart distracting worries and fears. Repeat the words of a desperate father: "I believe; help my unbelief" (Mark 9:24). When you feel the temptation of the evil one, say with all boldness in Christ, "Get behind me, Satan!" (Mark 8:33).

In close connection with your worry about earthly things will naturally be the daily labor you are called to do. God, of course, does not want you to be lazy in your work. On the contrary, He insists that you be a model of diligence and faithful service. But your work must not occupy your thoughts to the exclusion of spiritual and heavenly matters. After all, the sunshine that has its source in God's grace and Christ's redemption should glorify all you think and do, and as you approach His Table, you should seek to center your thoughts and desires on Him and do your utmost to turn them away from your daily work so that you do not lose that rest and peace for your soul that Christ has gained for you by His work on the cross and that He wishes to communicate to you in the Sacrament.

In particular, pray to the Lord that He would give you the desire and strength to drive out thoughts about sinful things and activities. Let your thoughts turn toward Calvary, and there, at the foot of the cross, kneel in deep humility and contrition, resting your eyes on the bleeding head, sad countenance, and tear-dimmed eyes of our blessed Savior as He suffers and dies there for your sins and the sins of the whole world. And as you do so, may this sight drive away every thought of earthly pleasure from your hearts and banish every sinful temptation in your mind! While there are many pleasures and pastimes that are harmless in themselves, they become positively harmful if you permit them to dominate you. Pray that the Lord will strengthen you in moments of weakness and temptation.

Another obstacle to receiving the Sacrament beneficially is a heart filled with hate, anger, and malice toward others. It should not be necessary to have your attention called to the fact that a heart filled with hatred and similar thoughts is closed to the benefits of Holy Communion; for in the very nature of things, it must be apparent that a heart filled with enmity and hatred has in it no room for the love of Christ. On the contrary, it must be apparent to everybody that such a heart is ruled by the thoughts and desires of an unworthy communicant, who will eat and drink damnation on himself. Christ cannot possibly welcome you to His Table if enmity instead of love fills your heart; for if you come to Holy Communion, which is the feast of His love, in a spirit of hatred and implacability, you make a mockery of Him whose love for you and whose longing for your forgiveness led Him to give His body and shed His blood on Calvary's cross. Always remember that one of the main purposes of Christ in instituting this Sacrament was that by the communion of His body and blood you might be more closely bound together by the mutual bond of love in Him whose love constrained Him to give Himself as a sacrifice for us. Yes, you who in the Holy Supper partake of the sacrifice of your Savior's love for the strengthening of your faith and thereby become most intimately united with Him and with others, how could you possibly harbor hatred and enmity in your heart toward those with whom you have become one or toward anyone whom Christ has redeemed by His blood? No, no; as you approach the altar, remember that Jesus commands us to love one another and forgive one another. The sad fate of the unforgiving servant who lost his master's forgiveness by his refusal to cancel the debt his fellow servant owed him in the parable should ever be a warning. Another warning is part of your daily prayer: "Forgive us our trespasses as we forgive those who trespass against us." Therefore, pray God to help you overcome all anger and enmity toward your neighbor for the sake of Christ's love to you. When you feel hateful thoughts, immediately pray for forgiveness and for the Holy Spirit to help you overcome those thoughts. Repent of them and look again to the love of Christ for you, and then you will recognize in all humility that you are not worthy of His love but that He loves you with a love inexpressible—and so also you extend forgiveness to others.

Finally, what can you do when you feel doubt about your worthiness to receive Holy Communion? Here, the point is not that you are sinful. You know you are. You confess that sin. You have repented and have been forgiven by Christ. But what if you feel timid and hesitant, wondering if indeed you are "sorry enough" for your sins? What about when you realize how weak your faith is and when you recognize doubts in your life? The Supper is precisely for those who are heavy-laden. Your doubts, your feelings that change from day to day, must not deter you from going to Jesus for His great mercy given to you in His Holy Meal. Your sins are never greater than Jesus' redemption. Hold fast to His mercy! Cling to your Lord and His great salvation. His mercy does not depend in any way on how you feel about it. His promises are always stronger than your doubt. His strength is always stronger than even your greatest fear and hesitancy. God's Word is clear in telling you that, as great as your sin may be, God's grace is much greater and that though your sins be as scarlet, they shall be as white as snow. When your heart trembles with worry, doubt, fear, or spiritual anguish, there is nothing better for you to do than cling to what John says: "If anyone does sin, we have an advocate with the Father, Jesus Christ the righteous" (1 John 2:1). Never forget that it is precisely to you, and all like you who are groaning under the burden of their sins, that Jesus gives this assurance: "Come to Me, all who labor and are heavy laden, and I will give you rest" (Matthew 11:28). Yes, it is you, at these times above all other times, whom Jesus tenderly invites to come to His Table.

PRAYER

Lord Jesus, as I approach Your Table, I find my mind not as free from earthly concerns as it should be, and these earthly matters greatly disturb my devotion and threaten to deprive me of Your heavenly blessings as offered to me in the Sacrament. To my great distress, I also see that in my heart there is not that full desire to forgive those who have wronged me, as should be found in a Christian's heart. And I likewise find that my contrition is not as deep as it should be and my hatred of sin is far from perfect. But because of my imperfections, I come to You for grace, forgiveness, and strength. O blessed Savior, grant me grace to prize the treasures You would bestow on me by Your flesh and blood in the Sacrament as immeasurably more precious than all the satisfaction that the world can give me; tear out all bitterness and enmity from my heart and make me meek and loving and forgiving; overcome my doubts by the assurances of Your Word and Sacrament; and fill my soul with a longing for the heavenly food and drink to which You have so graciously invited me. Yes, Lord Jesus, make me truly hungry and thirsty for Your grace, and then grant me sweet refreshment at Your Table for Your mercy's sake. Amen.

"I Believe; Help My Unbelief"
Mark 9:24

Faith in Christ is always clothed with humility. The higher the thoughts a person has of Christ, the lower the thoughts he will have of himself. If honest with yourself, you, too, know your own nothingness. But by the grace of God, your eyes will be opened to see the holiness and excellencies of your Lord Jesus. The knowledge that your own righteousness and merit are worth nothing in the eyes of a just God is used by the Holy Spirit to direct you to the Lamb of God, who takes away the sin of the world, and to assure you that forgiveness can be had only by appropriating Christ's sufferings, death, and atonement. This all-important truth will then bring home to you the fact that the guest who is welcome at the Lord's Table is the repentant sinner who trusts in Jesus' words: "Given . . . [and] shed for the forgiveness of your sins" (*LSB*, p. 162). Be cautious, however: while you must humbly recognize your sin, you must not focus so entirely on your sinful condition that Satan can use your honest introspection as a way to have you doubt that you are welcome to commune. While you are fully aware that you, by nature, are indeed most sinful and unclean, yet this conviction of your unworthiness must not tempt you to reject the clothing of Jesus' righteousness, which He gives you as He brings you into His heavenly banquet of salvation. The Holy Spirit in the Sacrament works in you both to will and to do His good pleasure. Jesus, in His free mercy, gives you the very help you need. Gratefully accept the righteousness of God in Him, and rejoice as Christ gives you the glorious dress of His blood and righteousness. Look to Christ as your perfect atoning sacrifice. Live in the glorious imputed righteousness and strength He gives you! Trust in His assurances! Your Savior is with you every day and comes to your aid to give you strength.

You can rejoice to know that the very body that was given and crucified and the very blood that was shed for your redemption are truly present and given to you to eat and drink under the consecrated bread and wine. Throw away any doubt that you are unworthy. Instead, look to Jesus and His great love. Focus on His omnipotence, omnipresence, faithfulness, wisdom, and truth. He gives you His body and blood in the Sacrament as a pledge of His forgiveness, as He has promised.

Hold fast to this blessed truth: Christ's sacrifice of His body and blood for the sins of the world was accepted by the Father as full atonement for your sins. In the Holy Supper, your heavenly Father imputes to you the merits of Christ's body and blood just as certainly as He gives you His Son's body and blood in the Sacrament. This is the specific purpose of the Lord's Supper, to assure you that all the blessings of Christ's redemption, forgiveness of sins, life, and salvation, are yours just as certainly as you receive the body and blood of the Lamb of God, who was slain for you. Your faith is founded on the perfect, holy, inerrant, and infallible Word of God, which stands firmer than the everlasting hills; for heaven and earth may pass away, but God's Word never will pass away. And even when Satan tries to induce you to imagine, in a spirit of false humility and lowliness, that your sins are greater than God's mercy can possibly be, do not succumb to such temptation, but rather overcome it by firmly clinging to and building on the promises of God's Word.

PRAYER

"[Lord,] I believe; help my unbelief" (Mark 9:24). So I feel constrained to cry as I am about to approach Your Table. As the searcher of hearts, You know that my faith is very weak and that doubts often disturb my thoughts. But, dear Lord Jesus, I cling to Your Word and rest in Your omnipotence and truth. I ever have before me Your assurance that in the Sacrament Your body and blood are given me and, further, that they are given me for the remission of my sins. I come to Your Table in full confidence that You will hold communion with me, as You have promised. Help me in an increasing measure to appreciate the glory of Your grace in the Sacrament and to drink with ever greater satisfaction the cup of salvation that You have purchased with Your blood and sweetened with Your blessing. Hear me, Lord Jesus, hear me, for Your own sake. Amen.

"Oh Give Thanks to The Lord, for He Is Good!"

Psalm 118:1

Give the Lord thanks, and express your gratitude by both your words and actions. Highly esteem your Redeemer and His blood and righteousness, through which such inestimably great blessings have been purchased for you. Avoid everything that dishonors Him, and flee from sin as you would from a plague. Commend your Redeemer to those who do not know Him by bearing witness of Him and of His truth and grace in the midst of a Christ-despising generation. Pray and work for the enlarging of Christ's kingdom, and rejoice at every victory your King Jesus wins over the powers of darkness.

Show your gratitude by singing psalms and hymns and spiritual songs in praise of Christ's redeeming love, His person, and His offices. Sing praises to the great God who left His throne on high and came down to dwell in the flesh to die for you, and magnify the glory of Him who rose from the dead for your justification and ascended to glory in heaven to take possession of His inheritance and to make intercession for you. This singing of praises to your Savior King is most acceptable to God and profitable to you. "Sing praises to God, sing praises! Sing praises to our King, sing praises!" (Psalm 47:6). God makes the singing of praises the eternal employment of the saints in heaven. Give thanks to God for His unspeakable gifts now and forever!

PRAYER

Blessed Jesus, in deepest humility and heartfelt gratitude, I give thanks to You that You have granted me, a poor sinner, the privilege of sitting at Your Table; that there You have nourished me with Your body and refreshed me with Your blood; and that You have made me an acceptable guest by clothing me, through Your Holy Spirit, with the wedding garment of faith in Your merits. O Lord, I confess that I am wholly unworthy of all the blessings You have bestowed on me in Your Sacrament; but the more deeply do I appreciate Your goodness, and the more earnestly am I concerned about giving You due thanks for Your great condescension and grace. Gracious Savior, accept the offerings of my lips and do not despise the gratitude of my inmost heart. I am truly grateful to You for Your atoning death and for Your merits, which You have so graciously imputed to me by faith as I partook of Your body and blood in the Sacrament. For all Your mercies I praise Your holy name. Blessed are You for having filled the hungry with good things and for having quenched the thirst of my soul. I dedicate my whole life to You and Your service. I shall count lost that day on which I forget Your love. Help me to grow in faith and love and hope. Deign to make me Your temple, and grant me strength to consecrate all my powers to Your service. Hear me for Your name's sake. Amen.

A Communion Meditation
and Prayer

Dear Lord Jesus, as I approach Your Table, help me think of all my needs and wants and so help me lay them before You. I humbly pray that out of Your fullness You will grant grace upon grace.

What I most of all desire is the full forgiveness of all my sins. When I think of my transgressions, I am ashamed to lift up my face to You; for against You have I sinned most grievously in thought, word, and deed. My transgressions are more than can be numbered. Which of Your commandments have I not broken? In what hour of my life have I not offended You? When I think of all my sins, I can but exclaim with the psalmist: "Who can discern his errors? Declare me innocent from hidden faults" (Psalm 19:12). I am heartily sorry for all the sins I have committed against You, and I have nothing to plead in extenuation for my transgressions. There would be no peace and no hope for me if Your blood did not cleanse me from all sins. All my trust I place in Your grace and mercy as my Redeemer. I know I have often abused Your mercy in the past and am not worthy to apply again for the cleansing by Your blood, which I have so often treated with contempt and trodden under foot. And yet, what can I do, and where can I go but to You?

In Your Word, you assure me that Your blood is able to wash away the stains of the deepest sins, and so I come to You and ask for the blessed power of Your blood on my soul. Lord, let it be to me according to Your Word. I pray that You look on my wretchedness and misery and have mercy on me for Your merits' sake. I have broken all the commandments of God; but You have kept them all in my stead. I have offended God's justice, despised His goodness, abused His patience, and deserved His wrath; but You were pierced for my transgressions and crushed for my iniquities; the chastisement of my peace was upon You, and therefore I trust that the merits of Your righteousness will be upon me. I flee to this city of refuge and lay hold of the horns of this altar and will not let You go until You bless me. And further I pray, though I am but dust and ashes: seal Your pardon to me by the communion of Your body and blood in the Sacrament, of which I am now to partake, that I may be able to exhibit it to Satan and my own accusing conscience and thus defy their attempts to deject and terrify me.

Without Your grace, I must languish and die. Without You, I can do nothing. I want to live by faith in You. Take possession of my heart and abide there. Lord, increase my faith; help my unbelief. May the Holy Sacrament of which I am about to partake be an earnest pledge that

You will grant my prayer. Grant that by faith I may place my finger into the mark of the nails that pierced Your hands and feet and place my hand into Your side, so that thus I may be fully persuaded that You have suffered and died for me. In mercy, grant me grace to say with Thomas, "My Lord and my God!" (John 20:28).

Lord Jesus, shed abroad Your warm love into my cold and frozen heart; inflame it with fervent affection and desire for You that I, too, may be a disciple whom You love and be numbered among those who love You in spirit and in truth.

Dear Lord, grant me also a greater measure of spiritual knowledge. You know that my mind is darkened by sin and I am naturally estranged from You through the ignorance that fills my heart. For want of keen spiritual sight, I am guilty of many mistakes. Give me understanding that I may know Your will; shine into my heart and give me an ever fuller knowledge of Your glorious self.

Give me also humility of spirit that I may not exalt myself above others. Keep my heart from swelling with foolish pride and vanity at every imagined or real honor or praise. And as I would have You graciously preserve me against haughtiness on the one hand, so also preserve me against insolence and worry at every disappointment. Lord Jesus, give me a greater portion of Your humility and meekness, and help me to imitate Your lowliness of spirit.

PRAYER

O Lord Jesus, do not grow impatient with me because of my constant asking. I must confess that I have not that deep sense and full conviction of my great sinfulness that I should have and wish to have, and therefore I ask You to give me more godly sorrow for sin. Remove my stony heart and give me a heart of flesh that I may despise myself for all my transgressions and iniquities. Give me greater purity of heart and a more spiritual mind that I may draw nearer to You and be more fit to be in Your presence. Grant me a greater hunger and a deeper thirst for righteousness. I know that You are more than willing to feed the hungry and give water to the thirsty, but I find that You must give me the hunger and thirst as well as the food and drink. Lord, give me this appetite and desire that I so greatly need just at this time as I am drawing near to Your Table. As the deer pants for the water brooks, so my soul pants for You, O Lord.

But my prayer is not yet ended. As I meditate on my wants, I find that I need more gratitude for all the mercies I have received from Your hands. Let me not be indifferent to Your food and drink, but grant me grace to show my appreciation for all Your loving kindnesses by satisfying my soul with the marrow and fatness Your grace sets before me at this banquet, and help my mouth praise You with joyful lips.

Grant me more patience and contentment in every

condition of life; give me more wisdom and prudence; bless me with greater courage and resolution; arouse me to greater activity and zeal. Cure my blindness, remove my impenitence, dispel my unbelief and hypocrisy, banish my deadness and formality, and replace my inconstancy and backslidings with firmness and loyalty.

O Lord, what is it that I do not need? But this is my comfort—I cannot want for anything that You cannot give me. Yes, You know what things I am in need of before I ask You, and You are able to do abundantly more than I can ask or think. Amen.

WHY YOU SHOULD RECEIVE
COMMUNION OFTEN

The apostle Paul complained that many of the Corinthian Christians did not make proper preparation before going to the Lord's Supper. Today, we must make the same complaint and add to it another, namely, that so many of our members commune so infrequently. We must deplore this irregular habit of taking Communion, and most of all deplore such tendencies in your own heart, mind, and soul. Let nothing keep you from the Lord's Supper! When your congregation makes it available, earnestly desire it and there present yourself at the Lord's Altar to receive the immeasurable blessing He gives you there.

But what should admonish and incite a Christian to receive the Sacrament frequently? Our Catechism answers this question: "First, both the command and the promise of Christ the Lord. Second, his own pressing need, because of which the command, encouragement, and promise are given" (Question 19).

Christ tells us in the Words of Institution of the Lord's Supper: "This do in remembrance of Me," and again: "This do, as often as you drink it, in remembrance of Me" $\left(LSB,\text{ p. 162}\right)$. Twice the Lord tells us: "This do." This repeated command should make it clear to you that going to the Holy Supper is not a matter of indifference, not a thing that we Christians may do or not do, as it may please us; for earnest and insistent is the divine command "This do." It makes it your sacred duty frequently to commune at the Lord's Table, even as His command makes it our joyful duty gladly to learn and hear His Word. The negligent and infrequent use of the Holy Sacrament in spite of this explicit command would be most reprehensible disobedience on your part and bring you great spiritual harm. But another reason why you should frequently commune is to be found in Christ's gracious promise. The believing communicant is promised indescribably glorious riches and blessings in the Lord's Supper. For hear what Christ says: "This is My body, which is given for you. . . . This cup is the new testament in My blood, which is shed for you for the forgiveness of sins" $\left(LSB,\text{ p. 162}\right)$. These words tell you that the Lord's Supper is a true love feast wherein Christ most wonderfully reveals His infinite love; a banquet of grace where Christ wishes to embrace you with His boundless grace; a heavenly table where He will give you a portion of eternal manna and a drink from the river of His pure pleasure. Every laboring and heavy-laden sinner is given these words to be assured of the Savior's love and mercy. To make you sure that all your sins really are forgiven, completely forgiven, and that life and salvation are yours, the Savior instituted this Holy Sacrament before His death as a memorial of His atoning sacrifice and as a pledge and token of your redemption. Because of Christ's promise, as found in these Words of Institution, you may say with full confidence: "As surely as Christ orally gives me in the Sacrament the very sacrifice He offered for my sins and the ransom He paid for my redemption, so certain am I that God is my gracious heavenly Father and heaven my eternal inheritance." In view of the glorious heavenly gifts and treasures offered and presented to you when you come trusting in His promise, why would you not wish to receive His Supper whenever you have the opportunity to do so?

But there is yet a third reason why you should be frequent guests at the Lord's Table, and that is the trouble of sin that lies heavily on you. As a Christian, you are still a sinner, and indeed, you daily sin much. So much and so seriously do you sin that it is impossible to have an idea of the number and greatness of these transgressions of God's Law. But your sins, even your sinful thoughts, are deserving of God's wrath and displeasure. And since such is the case, you stand in daily and continuous need of forgiveness; for which reason, you must often be assured: "Take heart, my son; your sins are forgiven" (Matthew 9:2). Of course, you have received forgiveness in Holy Baptism, and you are offered it in every Gospel sermon and in every absolution, but over and over again, you need to receive forgiveness in every form and manner the Lord provides it. Now, it is just because the blessed Savior foresaw this great need for constant reassurance that He, in His boundless love, instituted His Holy Supper, in which He assures you of the forgiveness of all your sins and thus strengthens your weak faith. And such being the case—in view of your weak faith and God's boundless love and His concern for your eternal welfare, which prompted Him to add this Sacrament to Baptism and the Gospel so that rest might be given to your troubled heart and confidence be brought to your trembling soul—should you not hasten to this blessed Table of God's grace to receive the priceless blessing that is intended for you? Should you not have a longing desire frequently to partake of this Sacrament and there to rid yourself of the heavy burden of sin?

May the Lord Jesus by His Holy Spirit lead you to be frequent and worthy guests at His Table, to be filled with a sincere longing for pardon and grace; and may He further grant you grace to leave His altar with the blessed assurance that your sins are forgiven!

PRAYER

O Lord, what am I that You should honor me? Give me a heart that will obediently heed Your command, and open my eyes to see the greatness of my sins and the riches of Your grace, so that I may frequently and gratefully accept Your invitation to partake of Your Holy Supper and rejoice to become a partaker of Your heavenly bounty—forgiveness of sins, light in darkness, comfort in sorrow, strength in weakness, help in distress, rest in labor, certainty in doubt, and protection in danger. Yes, Lord Jesus, let me taste in Your Supper Your heavenly goodness. Amen.

Counsel for the Sick and Dying

The benefits that Christ gives believing communicants make Communion a particular blessing for the sick to receive—and most certainly for those who are facing the end of their earthly days. Holy Communion in its very nature is a powerful means of strengthening the dying Christian's faith and assuring him of a blessed departure from this life. Since the believer is so intimately united with his Redeemer by partaking of His body and blood, this already is a pledge that Jesus will fulfill in him the promise that "where I am, there will My servant be also" (John 12:26). If you find yourself sick or on your deathbed, the Sacrament is for you a special blessing and gift.

You should realize that merely receiving Holy Communion, without faith, will bring no benefit. Do not think there is something "magical" about receiving the Lord's Supper when you are sick or death is near. No, remove any such false hope, but instead focus your heart and mind on the truths explained in this little book, pray the prayers, review the catechism and Christian Questions and Answers, and meditate on the penitential psalms and additional prayers at the back of this book.

Use the hymns provided to help you prepare for and rejoice in Holy Communion.

When you find yourself burdened with sickness or facing the last days of your earthly pilgrimage, bear in mind
that you must not postpone receiving the Sacrament. Before your mental strength has diminished, you should
turn your special attention to what has been your life
and conscientiously review it in the light of God's Law
and of our Savior's atoning death. May such a searching examination, with the help of the Holy Spirit, lead
you to sincere repentance and the honest desire to right
whatever wrong you have done, as much as lies in your
power. But may such heart searching also lead you to
Him who died that you may live forever and impel you
to take hold of Him as the safe anchor of hope amidst
the tempestuous seas of fear and doubt and accusations
that threaten to engulf you once your conscience is fully
awakened to realize the nature and consequences of your
disobedience. Cling to the Lord Jesus by trusting in His
Word and promises; do not permit Satan to lead you to
believe that Jesus is not willing to save you. Have no fear
that He will ever change His mind who said when He
was still here on earth in visible form: "Whoever comes
to Me I will never cast out" (John 6:37).

And when the Holy Spirit has brought you to such
a penitent and believing state of heart, permit nothing
to hold you back from the Lord's Table; for you will be

a most welcome guest, and great will be the blessings you will receive. By God's grace, you will experience, as you never did before, the sweet convictions that all your sins are forgiven and forgotten; that Jesus is your Savior, Guide, and Protector; that nothing can separate you from God's love in Christ Jesus; and that even before your departure from this life there is prepared for you a mansion in your heavenly Father's home.

PRAYER

Heavenly Father, according to Your will, I now find myself sick/dying. I know that You have only a kind and loving purpose in view in depriving me of my health, and willingly I bow to Your will and submit myself in patience to Your guidance.

I know that I have often sinned against Your will and deserved Your chastisement, but I come to You with a contrite and penitent heart and ask You graciously to forgive me for the sake of Jesus' merits. And that I may be the more certain of Your pardon, I desire to partake of my Savior's body and blood in the Sacrament. Gracious Father, I firmly believe that Your dear Son gave His body and shed His blood for the remission of my sins. By eating His body and drinking His blood, I desire to become more certain that all His merits are actually imputed to me, just as if I myself had suffered and died and atoned for my sins. Dearest Father, I believe this, but my own flesh and Satan seek to undermine my faith by instilling doubt into my heart. For this reason, I pray that You lay Your special blessing on my Communion that my weak faith may be strengthened as I receive this pledge and token of Your abiding love and mercy, which You have so graciously granted me in the Holy Supper.

Grant that my Communion may greatly contribute to my lasting blessing. Give me patience in suffering, courage under trials, comfort in sorrow, faith in temptation, certainty in doubt, and hope in despondency. Enable me in the strength of this heavenly food and drink to overcome all my enemies and, in the light of its blessed assurances, never to lose sight of my eternal goal.

Heavenly Father, I commit my body and soul with childlike confidence into Your gracious hands, since through Jesus' blood and redemption they have become Your own. I trustingly await the blessed hour when You will redeem me from these earthly toils and guide me into full and perfect liberty with all Christ's own in Your heaven of spotless purity and unalloyed bliss. O Father in heaven, keep me in this faith for Jesus' sake. Amen.

14

Additional Communion Prayers

ONE

Oh, the height, the depth, the length, and the breadth of Your love, O God! Angels cannot reach it; much less can human understanding fathom it. Only permit me, Lord, to look at it and wonder, to admire and adore that which I readily realize as being incomprehensible. Your love is a subject I do not know where to begin pondering; and once begun, I do not know where to end. Your love for us began long before we existed, long before the foundation of the world. Yes, Lord, You loved us when there was no eye to pity, even when we were less than nothing. Was there ever an eye enamored with deformity? Yet, when sin had so defiled us that from the crown of our head to the sole of our feet there was no soundness in us, You lovingly cast Your mantle over us to hide our shame. When we lay in our blood, expecting nothing but death, You said to us, "Live," and poured wine and oil into our wounds; You clothe us with white garments, deck us with jewels, graciously join us to Yourself, and receive us into Your bosom. So great was Your love for us that our extreme unworthiness could not abate it, but only increase and inflame it.

You commended Your love to us that, while we were yet sinners, Christ died for us. You pitied us when we hated You; and even when our hand was uplifted against You, Your arms were opened to receive and embrace us. Surely, never was love like Yours, not only passing knowledge, but wonder and admiration.

O Lord Jesus, I am lost in amazement when I see how Your love has drawn You toward us poor sinners! How unspeakable the love that could bring You down from the glory of the highest heavens and the bosom of Your eternal Father to this world, to this home of sorrow and death! How amazing Your love that could cause You to spend Your life, from the manger to the cross, in sorrow and grief that we might be happy! Your love is stronger than death and deeper than hell, higher than heaven, and longer than the earth. But not content with this manifestation of Your love, You do further in Your Supper give us a cup full of blessings, a good measure, pressed down, shaken together, and running over; nor is there fear of exhausting it. If we want pardon, here it is. If we want peace, it is there. If we want humility, patience, light, strength, comfort—all these gifts purchased by Christ with His blood He freely bestows on us in the Holy Supper as He gives us His body and blood. What is the manna that fed Israel in the wilderness, what is the water that gushed forth from the rock to quench their thirst, compared to this food and drink here offered to our souls? What is the pool of Bethesda, what are the waters of Siloam, to this blessed fountain, which cleanses from all sin and heals all spiritual diseases?

O Lord, what can I render to You for all these gifts of Your love? My love is so cold, and my services are so inadequate. I must blush that I am so sparing in my appreciation.

O Lord Jesus, take me just as I am and make me wholly Yours; grant me faith to expect, and patience to wait for, that hour when I shall stand before Your throne and serve You day and night in Your temple and when You shall take full possession of my heart and tune my lips to sing Your unending praise. Amen.

TWO

"My Lord and my God!" Only enable me to say that, and I ask no more, Lord Jesus. Others may think themselves happy that they can say, "My houses, my lands, my possessions, my treasures"; but, blessed Jesus, I shall deem myself unutterably rich and unspeakably happy if I may but lay hold on You as my Lord and my God. My life and happiness consist in this proprietorship. Life would be worth nothing to me if I could not say, "My Lord." There would be no comfort for me if You were not my God.

Now You come to me in Your Holy Sacrament and give me a sure pledge that You are mine. To support my tottering faith, You assure me that You are my Savior. To remove all doubt, You give me a token more sure than if You would permit me actually to put my finger into the prints of the nails and to thrust my hand into Your side. All this You do to prove that You are not only the founder but also the perfecter of my faith (see Hebrews 12:2), that You do not despise small things (see Psalm 119:141), that You will not break the bruised reed nor quench the smoldering wick (see Matthew 12:20), that You will pity the weakness of my faith, forgive my unbelieving and distrustful attitude, banish my guilty fears, confirm my wavering hopes, and enable me to say with well-grounded confidence, "My Lord and my God!" Hear me for Your mercy's sake. Amen.

THREE

Lord Jesus, no one but my God could know, no one but my Savior could forgive, my obstinate unbelief and come to my help as You do in the Holy Sacrament. I am astonished at my unbelief and at Your patience and long-suffering. I scarcely know which to wonder at most, the weakness of my faith or the strength of Your love. How surprising that You should stoop so low as to give me Your body and blood in Holy Communion to satisfy the needs of my wayward heart!

O Lord Jesus, I will have no God but You. No other Lord shall have dominion over me; and I humbly hope that no circumstance, however dark and discouraging, will ever again tempt me to question the power, the grace, or the faithfulness of my Lord and my God. As the body thirsts after the refreshing water, so grant that my soul may eagerly long for You. Amen.

FOUR

Dear Savior, I once again present myself at Your Table. Here, I have seen You in Your beauty; here, You have opened for me the treasures of Your grace and with rich variety satisfied me with good things. Here, You have, with no more apparent provision than a few loaves, fed many thousands that otherwise must have perished in the wilderness. In the breaking of bread, You have revealed Yourself to Your sorrowing disciples, to their inexpressible joy.

Here, therefore, I come in the humble hope of having closer fellowship with You, Lord Jesus. O You who can have compassion on the ignorant and those who have gone astray, cast me not away from Your presence. Do not send me away empty. Disperse the cloud that has separated me from You. Manifest Yourself to me so sweetly that I shall be forced to cry in faith and grateful admiration, "My Lord and my God." Amen.

FIVE

Blessed Jesus, Bread of Life, how many titles have You given Yourself to express Your love and tenderness to us and to bring home to us how much we poor and perishing sinners need! When we were full of wounds and putrefying sores, what we most wanted was a compassionate and skillful physician—one who could touch our infirmities and who was mighty to save. What sweet music to our souls is was to read of You: "He heals the broken hearted and binds up their wounds" (Psalm 147:3). When we were dead in sin and condemned to temporal death and eternal damnation, You gave peace to us with this blessed assurance: "I am the resurrection and the life. Whoever believes in Me, though he die, yet shall he live, and everyone who lives and believes in Me shall never die" (John 11:25–26). When we were distressed because of our sins and sought to flee from the presence of our "jealous and avenging God" (Nahum 1:2), You assured us that You are our mediator, ready to turn away the flames of God's wrath. When we were groping about like blind men, seeking God and not finding Him, You brought us these welcome tidings: "I am the way, and the truth, and the life. No one comes to the Father except through Me" (John 14:6). When we wandered about like lost sheep in the wilderness of this world's dangers and wants, without food and drink, You made our fainting hearts rejoice by telling us, "I am the good shepherd"

(John 10:11). These and many other titles You gave Yourself to tell us that all we need we can find in You. Grant me to find ever greater riches in You. To this end, bless my contemplated Communion. Amen.

SIX

Blessed Jesus, why did You show much greater love to us than to the angels? You show us favors the angels never knew. We are fed by Your love; You feed our hungry souls with good things. Like prodigals, we had left home, wasted our substance, and reduced ourselves to beggary and want; but here at Your Table, You give us Yourself as food for our souls; You are the most substantial refreshment. Pardon for sins, the favor of God, peace of conscience, a clean heart, a right spirit, grace to help, and the hope of glory are only some of the blessings You bring to us as we partake of Your body and Your blood in Your Supper. Yes, all we need is what You give us at Your Table, and thus You make us—who are poorer than Lazarus and full of sores—rich, well, and whole.

And now that You, Lord Jesus, have brought me into Your banqueting hall and set me at Your rich Table, I see all things are ready but myself. My heart is indifferent when it should rejoice. I am grieved and ashamed that my appetite is no keener in view of Your provisions; that You should set before me bread so nourishing, so strengthening, so enlivening but that I should be so list-less, as if I do not care whether I partake of it. I have long groaned under this melancholy ailment; I have often de-plored that my heart should be so sluggish and cold; I have labored to stir up more fervent desires; and now again I come to You and ask You to enable me to open my mouth wide and to enlarge the desires of my soul, to stir my heart to long after You and graciously to fill me with good things; then, O dearest Savior, shall a soul that was ready to perish bless Your holy name. Amen.

SEVEN

Dear Savior, with Your own lips, You have told us, "The Father Himself loves you" (John 16:27). The feast of Your Supper is proof sufficient of this love; for if He had not loved me, would He have done such great things for me through You? Would He have sent You into the world to save me? Would He have bruised You and put You to grief and made Your soul an offering for my sin? If He had not loved me, would He have called me and inclined and enabled me to heed the call to come? If He had not loved me, would He have brought me into His banquet hall? I was perishing with hunger, and all through my own fault; I had left His house and squan-dered His bounties; and if He had left me to starve, He would have done right, for I had done wickedly; but instead He rescued me from death, and now He bids me eat heavenly food such as is not given to angels. Yes, the evidences of His love are clear, but I so long to see more of the effects of His love and its influence on my heart. I would have my heart be more humbled and broken for sin. I wish to trust in God more implicitly. I wish my love to be more vigorous and fervent. I long to have Him who touched the mountains and made them smoke to touch my frozen heart with a live coal from His altar that, while I meditate on His amazing love to me, I may feel my love to Him kindled into a bright and living flame. I would not only profess my love and gratitude to Him, but I would also desire the strength to love Him in deed and in truth.

To this end, I am coming to my Savior's Table, which His and the Father's love has spread that Their love may be indelibly impressed on my heart, giving me strength to ward off all temptations of the devil, the world, and my own flesh. For I know that from the Lord's altar I shall have to go out again into the world, where this and that thing will entice me and where I shall meet with many things that will solicit my affections. When such solicitations and temptations beset me, let me hear You whispering to my heart as You remind me of Your Passion and its memorial, "Do you love Me more than these?" (John 21:15), and thus keep me from falling.

O Lord Jesus, grant that my Communion may be the

means to direct my heart into the love of You and the Father more and more. You have loved me and have always given me consolation and good hope through Your grace; now, comfort my heart and establish it in every good word and work for Your mercy's sake. Amen.

EIGHT

Blessed Savior, on the night when You ate the last Passover with Your disciples, You said to them: "I have earnestly desired to eat this Passover with you" (Luke 22:15). Such a desire to partake of the Holy Supper should fill my heart whenever the Table is spread. But have I this desire in the measure that it should be found in me? Dearest Savior, You know better than I can tell You that I must blush for shame because my desire is not greater than it is. Too often, other things come between You and me. For one thing, there is sin. O Lord, take away my iniquity and receive me graciously. Take all sin away, dear Lord; spare not a right hand or a right eye. Off with it! Out with it! There is no sin so dear to my sinful flesh that I will not sacrifice it by Your grace in order to come nearer to You. Another thing is the world. Teach me to see that the love of the world cannot live in the same heart with the love of my Savior. And another thing is doubt and unbelief, which so often spoil my appetite for Your Supper. I long after You, and yet there is a strange unwillingness within me—or shyness and distrust—to draw near to Your Table. I find my heart so dead, my thoughts so wandering, my love so cold. There are so many things in which I have sadly failed that I feel unworthy and fear that I may eat and drink judgment to myself. O dearest Jesus, make me ashamed of such unbelieving fears; do not let me insult Your love and goodness by doubting Your precious promises and by acting as if I thought You untrustworthy and Your Word not fit to be depended on. Teach me to put my whole trust in Your promises. Help me to say, "I am a poor helpless creature; where shall I go but to You, the Rock of Ages? I am a poor guilty creature; where shall I flee but to the Lamb of God, who takes away the sin of the world? I am a poor tempted creature; where shall I seek refuge but with my merciful and faithful High Priest, who, having been tempted in all things like as we are, can be touched by the feeling of my infirmities?" Lord, I flee to You; graciously receive me. Amen.

NINE

O Jesus, You have done all things possible to convince me of Your faithfulness. It was no worthiness in me that led You to make me the object of Your love at first; why should I think that Your love is not as free now as it was then? Lord Jesus, You have good reason to upbraid me for my doubts and indifference; for You have ever been ready to bear my griefs and carry my sorrows. Grant me grace humbly to throw myself at Your feet. Help me by Your mercy that my Communion may bring me ever nearer to You and that I may long ever more intensely for Your presence. Grant that, as I depart from Your Table, my heart may be enlarged and full in surrender to You; help that I may pray more earnestly for holiness, and make me strong successfully to overcome every temptation along my path with the strength that You are ready to give me at Your Table. Amen.

TEN

Lord, I come to Your Table not because I am worthy, but because You are rich in grace and promise that the needy shall not be forgotten and that the expectations of the poor shall not perish. I know that You will do as You have said: You will pity a poor, needy, perishing creature and fill me out of the ocean of Your mercy. As I come to the feast of Your appointment, You will not fail to display to me Your fullness and generosity. You will surely open the doors of Your treasury and allow me access to Your unsearchable riches. Your Word does assure me that in all ages You have bestowed these riches on the poor and needy without money and without price. Let me not go away from Your Table without alms, seeing there is bread enough and to spare. Let me not return from Your fountain of blessing unrefreshed! You have promised to pour water on the thirsty and floods on the dry ground; and see, Lord, there is no one more dry, more poor, more needy than I am. Lord, make me as thirsty as I am dry, as humble as I am poor, and as sensible as I am needy. Deal not with me according to my sense of need, which is small, but deal with me according to my actual wants and Your royal bounty, which is unlimited. Hear my humble prayer, dear Jesus. Amen.

ELEVEN

My Lord and Savior, oh, that I would feel my poverty and want as I should feel it: that I am drowned in debt to the Law and justice of God and have not one cent to pay it; that I am destitute of everything that is good and can do nothing to please God and am unworthy of the least of His mercies! Oh, that I could only be content to trust wholly in Your righteousness to justify me, and Your Spirit and grace to renew and sanctify my nature! Help me in my weakness, dear Savior. Amen.

TWELVE

Lord, I am poor, but in You are treasured up unsearchable riches and inexhaustible fullness to satisfy all my needs; I am naked, but You, Lord Jesus, have a robe of righteousness that is sufficient to cover me and a whole world of sinners; I am a starving creature, but You are the Bread of Life and the Water of Life for my soul; I am foolish and ignorant, but You have infinite wisdom to teach and guide me; I am laden with guilt, but Your sacrifice is sufficient to atone for it; I have strong lusts and desires, but You have a royal power to subdue them; I am in much darkness, but You are the Light of the world; I am under fears and discouragements, but You are the Consolation of Israel; I am wounded and sick, but You have balm to heal me; I am under a burden of debt, but You are my sure price, You are rich and fully able to pay; I am in prison, but You open the prison doors and loose my bonds; I am fatherless, but You are my everlasting Father; I am accused by the Law, Satan, and my own conscience, but You are my Advocate before the throne of divine justice. Therefore, I flee to You, Lord Jesus, for refuge and put my whole confidence in You. Amen.

THIRTEEN

O my Savior, what great encouragement it brings my needy soul that as a surety and pledge of Your goodness and merits You have instituted the Holy Sacrament, to which You most graciously invite me as a guest, thus preparing a table before me in the presence of all my enemies as an assurance that You will never leave me nor forsake me. Grant me grace to find at Your Table all the strength and comfort You have intended for me, for Your mercy's sake. Amen.

15

The Penitential Psalms

Psalm 6

¹ O Lord, rebuke me not in Your anger,
     nor discipline me in Your wrath.
² Be gracious to me, O Lord, for I am languishing;
     heal me, O Lord, for my bones are troubled.
³ My soul also is greatly troubled.
     But You, O Lord—how long?
⁴ Turn, O Lord, deliver my life;
     save me for the sake of Your steadfast love.
⁵ For in death there is no remembrance of You;
     in Sheol who will give You praise?
⁶ I am weary with my moaning;
     every night I flood my bed with tears;
     I drench my couch with my weeping.
⁷ My eye wastes away because of grief;
     it grows weak because of all my foes.
⁸ Depart from me, all you workers of evil,
     for the Lord has heard the sound of my
     weeping.
⁹ The Lord has heard my plea;
     the Lord accepts my prayer.

¹⁰ All my enemies shall be ashamed and greatly troubled;
    they shall turn back and be put to shame in
    a moment.

PSALM 32

¹ Blessed is the one whose transgression is forgiven,
    whose sin is covered.
² Blessed is the man against whom the LORD counts
no iniquity,
    and in whose spirit there is no deceit.
³ For when I kept silent, my bones wasted away
    through my groaning all day long.
⁴ For day and night Your hand was heavy upon me;
    my strength was dried up as by the heat of
    summer.
⁵ I acknowledged my sin to you,
    and I did not cover my iniquity;
I said, "I will confess my transgressions to the LORD,"
    and You forgave the iniquity of my sin.
⁶ Therefore let everyone who is godly
    offer prayer to You at a time when You may
    be found;
surely in the rush of great waters,
    they shall not reach him.

⁷You are a hiding place for me;
>   You preserve me from trouble;
>   You surround me with shouts of deliverance.
⁸I will instruct you and teach you in the way you
should go;
>   I will counsel you with My eye upon you.
⁹Be not like a horse or a mule, without understanding,
>   which must be curbed with bit and bridle,
>   or it will not stay near you.
¹⁰Many are the sorrows of the wicked,
>   but steadfast love surrounds the one who
>   trusts in the LORD.
¹¹Be glad in the LORD, and rejoice, O righteous,
>   and shout for joy, all you upright in heart!

PSALM 38

¹O LORD, rebuke me not in Your anger,
>   nor discipline me in Your wrath!
²For Your arrows have sunk into me,
>   and Your hand has come down on me.
³There is no soundness in my flesh
>   because of Your indignation;
there is no health in my bones
>   because of my sin.

4 For my iniquities have gone over my head;
    like a heavy burden, they are too heavy for me.
5 My wounds stink and fester
    because of my foolishness,
6 I am utterly bowed down and prostrate;
    all the day I go about mourning.
7 For my sides are filled with burning,
    and there is no soundness in my flesh.
8 I am feeble and crushed;
    I groan because of the tumult of my heart.
9 O Lord, all my longing is before You;
    my sighing is not hidden from You.
10 My heart throbs; my strength fails me,
    and the light of my eyes—it also has gone
    from me.
11 My friends and companions stand aloof from my
plague,
    and my nearest kin stand far off.
12 Those who seek my life lay their snares;
    those who seek my hurt speak of ruin
    and meditate treachery all day long.
13 But I am like a deaf man; I do not hear,
    like a mute man who does not open his
    mouth.
14 I have become like a man who does not hear,
    and in whose mouth are no rebukes.

[15] But for You, O Lord, do I wait;
     it is You, O Lord my God, who will answer.
[16] For I said, "Only let them not rejoice over me,
     who boast against me when my foot slips!"
[17] For I am ready to fall,
     and my pain is ever before me.
[18] I confess my iniquity;
     I am sorry for my sin.
[19] But my foes are vigorous, they are mighty,
     and many are those who hate me wrongfully.
[20] Those who render me evil for good
     accuse me because I follow after good.
[21] Do not forsake me, O Lord!
     O my God, be not far from me!
[22] Make haste to help me,
     O Lord, my salvation!

PSALM 51

[1] Have mercy on me, O God,
     according to Your steadfast love;
according to Your abundant mercy
     blot out my transgressions.
[2] Wash me thoroughly from my iniquity,
     and cleanse me from my sin!

3 For I know my transgressions,
      and my sin is ever before me.
4 Against You, You only, have I sinned
      and done what is evil in Your sight,
so that You may be justified in Your words
      and blameless in Your judgment.
5 Behold, I was brought forth in iniquity,
      and in sin did my mother conceive me.
6 Behold, You delight in truth in the inward being,
      and You teach me wisdom in the secret heart.
7 Purge me with hyssop, and I shall be clean;
      wash me, and I shall be whiter than snow.
8 Let me hear joy and gladness;
      let the bones that You have broken rejoice.
9 Hide Your face from my sins,
      and blot out all my iniquities.
10 Create in me a clean heart, O God,
      and renew a right spirit within me.
11 Cast me not away from Your presence,
      and take not Your Holy Spirit from me.
12 Restore to me the joy of Your salvation,
      and uphold me with a willing spirit.
13 Then I will teach transgressors Your ways,
      and sinners will return to You.
14 Deliver me from bloodguiltiness, O God,
      O God of my salvation,
      and my tongue will sing aloud of Your
      righteousness.

¹⁵ O Lord, open my lips,
  and my mouth will declare Your praise.
¹⁶ For You will not delight in sacrifice, or I would give it;
  You will not be pleased with a burnt offering.
¹⁷ The sacrifices of God are a broken spirit;
  a broken and contrite heart, O God, You will
  not despise.
¹⁸ Do good to Zion in Your good pleasure;
  build up the walls of Jerusalem;
¹⁹ then will You delight in right sacrifices,
  in burnt offerings and whole burnt offerings;
  then bulls will be offered on Your altar.

PSALM 102

¹ Hear my prayer, O LORD;
let my cry come to You!
² Do not hide Your face from me
  in the day of my distress!
Incline Your ear to me;
  answer me speedily in the day when I call!
³ For my days pass away like smoke,
  and my bones burn like a furnace.
⁴ My heart is struck down like grass and has withered;
  I forget to eat my bread.

⁵ Because of my loud groaning
       my bones cling to my flesh.
⁶ I am like a desert owl of the wilderness,
       like an owl of the waste places;
⁷ I lie awake;
       I am like a lonely sparrow on the housetop.
⁸ All the day my enemies taunt me;
       those who deride me use my name for a curse.
⁹ For I eat ashes like bread
       and mingle tears with my drink,
¹⁰ because of Your indignation and anger;
       for you have taken me up and thrown me
       down.
¹¹ My days are like an evening shadow;
       I wither away like grass.
¹² But You, O Lᴏʀᴅ, are enthroned forever;
       You are remembered throughout all
       generations.
¹³ You will arise and have pity on Zion;
       it is the time to favor her;
       the appointed time has come.
¹⁴ For Your servants hold her stones dear
       and have pity on her dust.
¹⁵ Nations will fear the name of the Lᴏʀᴅ,
       and all the kings of the earth will fear
       Your glory.

¹⁶ For the LORD builds up Zion;
  He appears in His glory;
¹⁷ He regards the prayer of the destitute
  and does not despise their prayer.
¹⁸ Let this be recorded for a generation to come,
   so that a people yet to be created may praise
   the LORD
¹⁹ that He looked down from His holy height;
   from heaven the LORD looked at the earth,
²⁰ to hear the groans of the prisoners,
   to set free those who were doomed to die,
²¹ that they may declare in Zion the name of the LORD,
   and in Jerusalem His praise,
²² when peoples gather together,
   and kingdoms, to worship the LORD.
²³ He has broken my strength in midcourse;
  He has shortened my days.
²⁴ "O my God," I say, "take me not away
  in the midst of my days—
You whose years endure
  throughout all generations!"
²⁵ Of old You laid the foundation of the earth,
  and the heavens are the work of Your hands.
²⁶ They will perish, but You will remain;
  they will all wear out like a garment.
You will change them like a robe,
  and they will pass away,

²⁷ but You are the same, and Your years have no end.
²⁸ The children of Your servants shall dwell secure;
       their offspring shall be established before You.

PSALM 130

¹ Out of the depths I cry to You, O LORD!
      ² O Lord, hear my voice!
Let Your ears be attentive
      to the voice of my pleas for mercy!
³ If You, O LORD, should mark iniquities,
      O Lord, who could stand?
⁴ But with You there is forgiveness,
      that You may be feared.
⁵ I wait for the LORD, my soul waits,
      and in His word I hope;
⁶ my soul waits for the Lord
      more than watchmen for the morning,
      more than watchmen for the morning.
⁷ O Israel, hope in the LORD!
      For with the LORD there is steadfast love,
      and with Him is plentiful redemption.
⁸ And He will redeem Israel
      from all his iniquities.

PSALM 143

¹ Hear my prayer, O LORD;
            give ear to my pleas for mercy!
            In Your faithfulness answer me, in Your
            righteousness!
² Enter not into judgment with Your servant,
            for no one living is righteous before You.
³ For the enemy has pursued my soul;
            he has crushed my life to the ground;
            he has made me sit in darkness like those
            long dead.
⁴ Therefore my spirit faints within me;
            my heart within me is appalled.
⁵ I remember the days of old;
            I meditate on all that You have done;
            I ponder the work of Your hands.
⁶ I stretch out my hands to You;
            my soul thirsts for You like a parched land.
⁷ Answer me quickly, O LORD!
            My spirit fails!
Hide not Your face from me,
            lest I be like those who go down to the pit.
⁸ Let me hear in the morning of Your steadfast love,
            for in You I trust.
Make me know the way I should go,
            for to You I lift up my soul.

9 Deliver me from my enemies, O LORD!
    I have fled to You for refuge.
10 Teach me to do Your will,
    for You are my God!
Let Your good Spirit lead me
    on level ground!
11 For Your name's sake, O LORD, preserve my life!
    In Your righteousness bring my soul out of
    trouble!
12 And in Your steadfast love You will cut off my enemies,
    and You will destroy all the adversaries of my
        soul,
    for I am Your servant.

16

Communion Hymns

O Lord, We Praise Thee

LSB 617
German, 14th century, stanza 1
Martin Luther, stanzas 2–3

1. O Lord, we praise Thee, bless Thee, and adore Thee,
    In thanksgiving bow before Thee.
    Thou with Thy body and Thy blood didst nourish
    Our weak souls that they may flourish:
      O Lord, have mercy!
    May Thy body, Lord, born of Mary,
    That our sins and sorrows did carry,
    And Thy blood for us plead
    In all trial, fear, and need:
      O Lord, have mercy!

2. Thy holy body into death was given,
    Life to win for us in heaven.
    No greater love than this to Thee could bind us;
    May this feast thereof remind us!
      O Lord, have mercy!
    Lord, Thy kindness did so constrain Thee
    That Thy blood should bless and sustain me.
    All our debt Thou hast paid;

Peace with God once more is made:
> O Lord, have mercy!

3. May God bestow on us His grace and favor
That we follow Christ our Savior
And live together here in love and union
Nor despise this blest Communion!
> O Lord, have mercy!

Let not Thy good Spirit forsake us;
Grant that heav'nly-minded He make us;
Give Thy Church, Lord, to see
Days of peace and unity:
> O Lord, have mercy!

I COME, O SAVIOR, TO THY TABLE

LSB 618
Friedrich Christian Heyder

1. I come, O Savior, to Thy table,
> For weak and weary is my soul;
Thou, Bread of Life, alone art able
> To satisfy and make me whole:
Refrain: Lord, may Thy body and Thy blood
> Be for my soul the highest good!

2. Thy heart is filled with fervent yearning
   That sinners may salvation see
   Who, Lord, to Thee in faith are turning;
   So I, a sinner, come to Thee. *Refrain.*

3. Unworthy though I am, O Savior,
   Because I have a sinful heart,
   Yet Thou Thy lamb wilt banish never,
   For Thou my faithful shepherd art: *Refrain.*

4. Weary am I and heavy laden;
   With sin my soul is sore oppressed;
   Receive me graciously and gladden
   My heart, for I am now Thy guest. *Refrain.*

5. What higher gift can we inherit?
   It is faith's bond and solid base;
   It is the strength of heart and spirit,
   The covenant of hope and grace. *Refrain.*

THY BODY, GIVEN FOR ME, O SAVIOR

LSB 619
Friedrich Christian Heyder

1. Thy body, giv'n for me, O Savior,
   Thy blood which Thou for me didst shed,

These are my life and strength forever,
    By them my hungry soul is fed.
Refrain: Lord, may Thy body and Thy blood
    Be for my soul the highest good!

2. With Thee, Lord, I am now united;
    I live in Thee and Thou in me.
No sorrow fills my soul, delighted
    It finds its only joy in Thee. *Refrain.*

3. Who can condemn me now? For surely
    The Lord is nigh, who justifies.
No hell I fear, and thus securely
    With Jesus I to heaven rise. *Refrain.*

4. Though death may threaten with disaster,
    It cannot rob me of my cheer;
For He who is of death the master
    With aid and comfort e'er is near. *Refrain.*

5. My heart has now become Thy dwelling,
    O blessèd, holy Trinity.
With angels I, Thy praises telling,
    Shall live in joy eternally. *Refrain.*

LORD JESUS CHRIST, YOU HAVE PREPARED

LSB 622
Samuel Kinner; tr. Emmanuel Cronenwett

1. Lord Jesus Christ, You have prepared
      This feast for our salvation;
   It is Your body and Your blood,
      And at Your invitation
   As weary souls, with sin oppressed,
   We come to You for needed rest,
      For comfort, and for pardon.

2. Although You did to heaven ascend,
      Where angel hosts are dwelling,
   And in Your presence they behold
      Your glory, all excelling,
   And though Your people shall not see
   Your glory and Your majesty
      Till dawns the judgment morning,

3. Yet, Savior, You are not confined
      To any habitation;
   But You are present even now
      Here with Your congregation.
   Firm as a rock this truth shall stand,
   Unmoved by any daring hand
      Or subtle craft and cunning.

4. We eat this bread and drink this cup,
      Your precious Word believing
   That Your true body and Your blood
      Our lips are here receiving.
   This Word remains forever true;
   All things are possible with You,
      For You are Lord Almighty.

5. Though reason cannot understand,
      Yet faith this truth embraces:
   Your body, Lord, is even now
      At once in many places.
   I leave to You how this can be;
   Your Word alone suffices me;
      I trust its truth unfailing.

6. Lord, I believe what You have said;
      Help me when doubts assail me.
   Remember that I am but dust,
      And let my faith not fail me.
   Your supper in this vale of tears
   Refreshes me and stills my fears
      And is my priceless treasure.

7. Grant that we worthily receive
      Your supper, Lord, our Savior,
   And, truly grieving for our sins,
      May prove by our behavior

That we are thankful for Your grace
And day by day may run our race,
   In holiness increasing.

8. For Your consoling supper, Lord,
   Be praised throughout all ages!
Preserve it, for in ev'ry place
   The world against it rages.
Grant that this sacrament may be
A blessèd comfort unto me
   When living and when dying.

Public domain

LORD JESUS CHRIST, LIFE-GIVING BREAD

LSB 625
Johann Rist; tr. Arthur T. Russell

1. Lord Jesus Christ, life-giving bread,
   May I in grace possess You.
Let me with holy food be fed,
   In hunger I address You.
Prepare me well for You, O Lord,
And, humbly by my prayer implored,
   Give me Your grace and mercy.

2. To pastures green, Lord, safely guide,
   To restful waters lead me;
Your table well for me provide,
   Your wounded hand now feed me.

Though weary, sinful, sick, and weak,
Refuge in You alone I seek,
    To share Your cup of healing.

3. O bread of heaven, my soul's delight,
        For full and free remission
    I come with prayer before Your sight
        In sorrow and contrition.
    Your righteousness, Lord, cover me
    That I receive You worthily,
        Assured of Your full pardon.

4. I do not merit favor, Lord,
        My weight of sin would break me;
    In all my guilty heart's discord,
        O Lord, do not forsake me.
    In my distress this comforts me
    That You receive me graciously,
        O Christ, my Lord of mercy!

Public domain

SOUL, ADORN YOURSELF WITH GLADNESS

LSB 636
Johann Franck

1. Soul, adorn yourself with gladness,
    Leave the gloomy haunts of sadness,
        Come into the daylight's splendor,
        There with joy your praises render.

Bless the One whose grace unbounded
This amazing banquet founded;
    He, though heavenly, high, and holy,
    Deigns to dwell with you most lowly.

2.   Hasten as a bride to meet Him,
And with loving reverence greet Him.
    For with words of life immortal
    He is knocking at your portal.
Open wide the gates before Him,
Saying, as you there adore Him:
    Grant, Lord, that I now receive You,
    That I nevermore will leave You.

3.   He who craves a precious treasure
Neither cost nor pain will measure;
    But the priceless gifts of heaven
    God to us has freely given.
Though the wealth of earth were proffered,
None could buy the gifts here offered:
    Christ's true body, for you riven,
    And His blood, for you once given.

4.   Now in faith I humbly ponder
Over this surpassing wonder
    That the bread of life is boundless
    Though the souls it feeds are countless:

With the choicest wine of heaven
Christ's own blood to us is given.
    Oh, most glorious consolation,
    Pledge and seal of my salvation!

5. Jesus, source of lasting pleasure,
Truest friend, and dearest treasure,
    Peace beyond all understanding,
    Joy into all life expanding:
Humbly now, I bow before You;
Love incarnate, I adore You;
    Worthily let me receive You
    And, so favored, never leave You.

6. Jesus, sun of life, my splendor,
Jesus, friend of friends, most tender,
    Jesus, joy of my desiring,
    Fount of life, my soul inspiring:
At Your feet I cry, my maker,
Let me be a fit partaker
    Of this blessèd food from heaven,
    For our good, Your glory, given.

7. Lord, by love and mercy driven,
You once left Your throne in heaven
    On the cross for me to languish
    And to die in bitter anguish,

To forego all joy and gladness
And to shed Your blood in sadness.
    By this blood redeemed and living,
    Lord, I praise You with thanksgiving.

8. Jesus, bread of life, I pray You,
    Let me gladly here obey You.
        By Your love I am invited,
        Be Your love with love requited;
    By this Supper let me measure,
    Lord, how vast and deep love's treasure.
        Through the gift of grace You give me
        As Your guest in heaven receive me.

Stanzas 1, 4–5 © 1978 *Lutheran Book of Worship*;
used by permission.
Stanzas 2–3, 6–8, public domain

O Living Bread from Heaven

LSB 642
Johann Rist; tr. Catherine Winkworth, alt.

1. O living Bread from heaven,
        How well You feed your guest!
    The gifts that You have given
        Have filled my heart with rest.
    Oh, wondrous food of blessing,
        Oh, cup that heals our woes!

My heart, this gift possessing,
   With praises overflows.

2. My Lord, You here have led me
   To this most holy place
And with Yourself have fed me
   The treasures of Your grace;
For You have freely given
   What earth could never buy,
The bread of life from heaven,
   That now I shall not die.

3. You gave me all I wanted;
   This food can death destroy.
And You have freely granted
   The cup of endless joy.
My Lord, I do not merit
   The favor You have shown,
And all my soul and spirit
   Bow down before Your throne.

4. Lord, grant me then, thus strengthened
   With heav'nly food, while here
My course on earth is lengthened,
   To serve with holy fear.
And when You call my spirit
   To leave this world below,
I enter, through Your merit,
   Where joys unmingled flow.

17

CHRISTIAN QUESTIONS
WITH THEIR ANSWERS

Prepared by Dr. Martin Luther for those who intend to go to the Sacrament. (The "Christian Questions with Their Answers," designating Luther as the author, first appeared in an edition of the Small Catechism in 1551.)

After confession and instruction in the Ten Commandments, the Creed, the Lord's Prayer, and the Sacraments of Baptism and the Lord's Supper, the pastor may ask, or Christians may ask themselves these questions:

1. **Do you believe that you are a sinner?**
   Yes, I believe it. I am a sinner.

2. **How do you know this?**
   From the Ten Commandments, which I have not kept.

3. **Are you sorry for your sins?**
   Yes, I am sorry that I have sinned against God.

4. **What have you deserved from God because of your sins?**
   His wrath and displeasure, temporal death, and eternal damnation. See Rom. 6:21, 23.

5. **Do you hope to be saved?**
   Yes, that is my hope.

6. **In whom then do you trust?**

   In my dear Lord Jesus Christ.

7. **Who is Christ?**

   The Son of God, true God and man.

8. **How many Gods are there?**

   Only one, but there are three persons: Father, Son, and Holy Spirit.

9. **What has Christ done for you that you trust in Him?**

   He died for me and shed His blood for me on the cross for the forgiveness of sins.

10. **Did the Father also die for you?**

    He did not. The Father is God only, as is the Holy Spirit; but the Son is both true God and true man. He died for me and shed His blood for me.

11. **How do you know this?**

    From the holy Gospel, from the words instituting the Sacrament, and by His body and blood given me as a pledge in the Sacrament.

12. **What are the words of institution?**

    Our Lord Jesus Christ, on the night when He was betrayed, took bread, and when He had given thanks, He broke it and gave it to the disciples and said: "Take eat; this is My body, which is given for you. This do in remembrance of Me."

    In the same way also He took the cup after supper, and when He had given thanks, He gave it to them, saying: "Drink of it, all of you; this cup is the new testament in My blood, which is shed for you for the forgiveness of sins. This do, as often as you drink it, in remembrance of Me."

13. Do you believe, then, that the true body and blood of Christ are in the Sacrament?

Yes, I believe it.

14. What convinces you to believe this?

The word of Christ: Take, eat, this is My body; drink of it, all of you, this is My blood.

15. What should we do when we eat His body and drink His blood, and in this way receive His pledge?

We should remember and proclaim His death and the shedding of His blood, as He taught us: This do, as often as you drink it, in remembrance of Me.

16. Why should we remember and proclaim His death?

First, so that we may learn to believe that no creature could make satisfaction for our sins. Only Christ, true God and man, could do that. Second, so we may learn to be horrified by our sins, and to regard them as very serious. Third, so we may find joy and comfort in Christ alone, and through faith in Him be saved.

17. What motivated Christ to die and make full payment for your sins?

His great love for His Father and for me and other sinners, as it is written in John 14; Romans 5; Galatians 2; and Ephesians 5.

18. Finally, why do you wish to go to the Sacrament?

That I may learn to believe that Christ, out of great love, died for my sin, and also learn from Him to love God and my neighbor.

19. **What should admonish and encourage a Christian to receive the Sacrament frequently?**

First, both the command and the promise of Christ the Lord. Second, his own pressing need, because of which the command, encouragement, and promise are given.

20. **But what should you do if you are not aware of this need and have no hunger and thirst for the Sacrament?**

To such a person no better advice can be given than this: first, he should touch his body to see if he still has flesh and blood. Then he should believe what the Scriptures say of it in Galatians 5 and Romans 7.

Second, he should look around to see whether he is still in the world, and remember that there will be no lack of sin and trouble, as the Scriptures say in John 15–16 and in 1 John 2 and 5.

Third, he will certainly have the devil also around him, who with his lying and murdering day and night will let him have no peace, within or without, as the Scriptures picture him in John 8 and 16; 1 Peter 5; Ephesians 6; and 2 Timothy 2.

Note: These questions and answers are no child's play, but are drawn up with great earnestness of purpose by the venerable and devout Dr. Luther for both young and old. Let each one pay attention and consider it a serious matter; for St. Paul writes to the Galatians in chapter six: "Do not be deceived: God cannot be mocked."